soufflés

soufflés

Sara Lewis

hamlyn

Notes

The FDA advises that eggs should not be consumed raw. This book contains some dishes made with raw or lightly cooked eggs. It is prudent for more vulnerable people such as pregnant and nursing mothers, invalids, the elderly, babies, and young children to avoid uncooked or lightly cooked dishes made with eggs.

Whole milk should be used unless otherwise stated.

Fresh herbs should be used unless otherwise stated.
Large eggs should be used unless otherwise stated.

Ovens should be preheated to the specified temperature—if using a fan-assisted oven, follow the manufacturer's instructions for adjusting the time and the temperature.

First published in Great Britain in 2005 by
Hamlyn, a division of Octopus Publishing Group Ltd
2–4 Heron Quays, London E14 4JP

ISBN 0 600 61264 3
EAN 9780600612643

A CIP catalog record for this book is available from the British Library

Printed and bound in China

10 9 8 7 6 5 4 3 2

contents

introduction

Soufflés may be baked and served straight from the oven, or uncooked and served chilled; they may also be sweet or savory. The one thing all soufflés have in common is a light, airy texture due to the inclusion of beaten egg whites.

The classic soufflé is the hot, baked version, which was originally developed in France as a means of using up leftover food (creatively combined with the household staples of eggs and flour). In cookery terms, this is the soufflé regarded with the greatest respect and the one that most people shy away from making. They eat them only when they order one in a restaurant, and watch, transfixed, when a television chef pulls a perfectly risen creation from the oven, smiling triumphantly and ignoring the 15 previous takes that didn't quite go according to plan! The baked souffle's tricky reputation derives from the fact that it relies on hot air to rise and so has a tendency to collapse as soon as it is removed from the oven.

This book will shatter the illusion of the impossible hot soufflé and show you that it's not actually that difficult to make one. All it takes is the right ingredients, the right techniques, and a little dash of confidence.

"The only thing that will make a soufflé fall is if it knows you are afraid of it."
James Beard

hot soufflés

A basic hot soufflé mixture consists of a thick base sauce (usually a roux-based white sauce for a savory soufflé or a crème pâtissière for a sweet one) mixed with beaten egg whites, to which can be added almost any savory or sweet flavoring—from cheese or chorizo to chocolate or fruit. The variations really are endless, as you'll discover from the recipes in this book.

Beat cheese into a hot, thick, roux-based white sauce with mustard and salt and pepper, and stir until the cheese has melted.

Off the heat, stir the egg yolks into the flavored sauce and beat until smooth.

Fold a large spoonful of beaten egg whites into the thick, cooled sauce to loosen the mixture, then gently fold in the remainder.

Gradually add dissolved gelatin in a thin, steady trickle to thickly beaten egg yolks and sugar.

Fold in flavorings such as puréed fruits or melted chocolate and softly whipped heavy cream.

Beat egg whites into stiff peaks, then fold a large spoonful into the cream mixture to loosen it. Gently fold in the remainder.

The mixture is spooned into a prepared soufflé dish and placed in a preheated oven. The trapped air in the beaten egg whites causes the soufflé to rise as it cooks. This accounts for its name, which loosely translates from the French *souffler* meaning "to blow up." At the end of the cooking time, a successful soufflé should emerge from the oven towering impressively above the rim of its mold, supported by a collar of paper tied around the dish with string. The soufflé is then served at once, still hot and wobbling, before it collapses.

chilled soufflés

These soufflés are mousse-like, sweet soufflés made with stiffly beaten, *uncooked* egg whites. This fact means that it is unwise to serve chilled soufflés to pregnant and nursing mothers, young children, and the elderly.

They usually include thick cream and gelatin among the ingredients and require chilling (or freezing) in order to set. A chilled soufflé also relies on a paper collar around the dish. This allows the mixture to set proud of its mold and is removed on serving to produce a striking dessert.

tips for successful soufflés

Measure out all your ingredients before you begin. This is good practice when following any recipe so you won't forget any of the ingredients or discover you're missing something halfway through.

• Line the dish for a hot soufflé with ingredients such as flour or bread crumbs (see page 8) to help the mixture rise as it cooks and prevent it from sticking to the sides of the mold. (The dish for a chilled soufflé does not need lining.)

• Make a paper collar (see page 8) for the soufflé dish to support the soufflé as it rises or sets.

• As with other recipes that use beaten egg whites—such as meringue—make sure your mixing bowl and whisk are clean and dry. If the bowl has been in the cupboard for a while, a quick wipe over is not sufficient: you'll need to wash and dry it carefully before use.

• For best results, chill your eggs in the refrigerator and separate them when they're still cold. However, allow the whites to come to room temperature before beating them, as this will help to increase the volume of your soufflé by incorporating more air.

• Don't over-beat the egg whites; they will become dry and it will be difficult to combine them with other ingredients.

• Use a plastic spatula when combining soufflé ingredients, and fold in the mixture as gently as possible.

• For soufflés that include gelatin in the ingredients, it's important to add this in a steady, continuous stream.

• Make sure the oven has reached the required temperature before you start to cook your soufflé. Place it in the center of the oven to cook and don't open the oven door to check on progress during cooking until almost at the end, as the temperature will drop and your soufflé might flop.

• Some hot soufflés can be prepared in advance and then chilled until the stiffly beaten egg whites are added just before baking. This is useful if you're preparing a hot soufflé for a dinner party, as you'll have only the final cooking to do at the last minute.

Lining a soufflé dish

1 To line a dish in preparation for a hot soufflé, grease the bottom and sides of the dish with butter and then sprinkle in a tablespoon of sugar or ground almonds (for sweet soufflés) or flour, bread crumbs, ground nuts, or grated cheese (for savory soufflés).

2 Tilt the dish and tap it gently, turning it around, so that your chosen ingredient covers the inside of the dish evenly.

3 Tip out any excess sugar, flour, or other ingredient being used for the lining.

Making a soufflé collar

1 To make a collar for a soufflé, cut a length of parchment paper (also known as baking parchment) slightly longer than the circumference of the soufflé dish. Fold it in half lengthwise so that it will be strong enough to support the soufflé.

2 Wrap the length of paper around the outside of the dish so that it stands higher than the top of the dish—no more than 3 inches. Fix in place securely with a length of string and knot tightly.

3 Just before serving, snip the string and carefully remove the paper collar.

Spread butter or olive oil over the bottom and sides of an ovenproof soufflé dish.

For a savory soufflé, sprinkle the bottom and sides of the dish with flour or bread crumbs, finely grated cheese, or ground nuts.

For a sweet soufflé, sprinkle the bottom and sides of the dish with superfine sugar, ground nuts, or flour, tilting the dish for even coverage.

Wrap a folded length of parchment paper around the dish so that the ends overlap and the paper stands between 1½ and 3 in high.

Tie the paper securely in place with fine string and snip off the ends.

When the soufflé has set (or cooked), snip off the string and peel away the paper, using a knife to prevent the soufflé edge from tearing.

equipment

Soufflés are not complicated dishes to cook, and therefore the list of necessary equipment is not long.

● **Soufflé dish** The most important thing to consider for hot soufflés is the actual soufflé dish. The ideal shape is cylindrical with straight, smooth sides so that the soufflé can rise easily and will not catch on the sides or between ridges. Soufflé dishes are ideally made of ovenproof porcelain, but whatever dish you use, it should be suitably heatproof. Depending on the recipe, you may require one large dish or a number of smaller dishes (known as ramekins) for individual servings. If you don't have a specific soufflé dish, soufflés can, in theory, be cooked in any straight-sided heatproof container—the important thing is to ensure that you use the correct size for the mixture. Five different sizes of soufflé dishes have been used for the recipes in this book, ranging from 3-inch diameter x 1½-inch deep individual soufflé dishes to a medium tall 6-inch diameter x 3¾-inch deep dish.

● **Mixing bowl** Use a stainless steel or glass mixing bowl when beating the eggs. It is easier to get these bowls absolutely clean—plastic can sometimes retain oil on its surface, which will prevent your egg whites from stiffening.

● **Whisk** You could use a hand whisk for beating the eggs, but an electric one will save you time and energy.

● **Additional items** You will also need parchment paper, a pair of scissors, and some string for soufflé collars, and oven mitts are essential for transferring a hot soufflé from the oven to the table as quickly as possible.

start souffléing!

Now that you know all there is to know about making soufflés, choose a recipe from among the following pages, buy the ingredients, and put a soufflé on the menu tonight. Try Black Olive and Basil Soufflés served with roasted tomatoes (page 17) for a light meal, Twice-Baked Cheese and Walnut Soufflés (page 24) for a special occasion, or how about the decadent White Choc Soufflés with Dark Chocolate Sauce (page 32) to indulge a sweet tooth? Once you've perfected the art of making soufflés, you could find yourself rustling one up every other day, whether for lunch or dinner!

hot savory
soufflés

triple-cheese soufflé with apple compote

5 tablespoons butter

1/3 cup freshly grated Parmesan
   cheese

1/2 cup grated strong cheddar cheese

3/4 cup grated Gruyère cheese

1/2 cup all-purpose flour

11/3 cups milk

1 teaspoon Dijon mustard

4 eggs, separated

large pinch of cayenne pepper

salt

green salad, to serve

Apple compote

1 tablespoon butter

2 dessert apples, cored and thickly
   sliced

1 tablespoon superfine sugar

1 tablespoon cider vinegar

4 tablespoons water

Serves 4
Preparation time: 30 minutes
Cooking time: 30–35 minutes

This rich, soft cheese soufflé contrasts well with the tangy sharpness of the warm apple compote to make a luxurious light lunch or supper dish. You could experiment if you like and make up your own triple-cheese combinations.

1 Grease a medium tall 6-inch diameter x 3³/4-inch deep soufflé dish with some of the butter. Mix the three cheeses together, then use 3 tablespoons to line the dish (see page 8). Attach a soufflé collar that stands 3 inches higher than the top of the dish (see page 8).

2 Melt the remaining butter in a pan, stir in the flour, and cook for 1 minute. Gradually mix in the milk and bring to a boil, stirring until thickened and smooth.

3 Stir in the remaining cheeses, mustard, egg yolks, cayenne pepper, and a little salt. Cover and let cool.

4 Beat the egg whites into stiff, moist-looking peaks. Fold a large spoonful into the cooled sauce to loosen the mixture, then fold in the remaining egg whites.

5 Pour the mixture into the prepared soufflé dish and bake in a preheated oven, 375°F, for 25–30 minutes until the soufflé is well risen, the top is browned, and there is a slight wobble to the center.

6 While the soufflé cooks, melt the butter for the compote in a small skillet, add the apples, and fry for 4–5 minutes until hot. Sprinkle with the sugar, cook for 2–3 minutes until just beginning to brown, then add the vinegar and water and simmer for 2–3 minutes until syrupy.

7 Quickly snip the string off the soufflé collar and gently peel away the paper. Spoon the soufflé onto plates. Serve with the apple compote and a green salad.

smoked salmon and dill soufflé

5 tablespoons butter

3 tablespoons fresh bread crumbs

1/2 cup all-purpose flour

11/3 cups milk

4 tablespoons full-fat crème fraîche or
sour cream

3 tablespoons chopped dill

grated zest of 1 lemon

4 eggs, separated

4 oz sliced smoked salmon, cut into
thin strips

salt and freshly ground black pepper

To serve

slices of smoked salmon (optional)

lemon wedges

Serves 4

Preparation time: 30 minutes

Cooking time: 35–40 minutes

1 Grease a medium tall 6-inch diameter x 3³/₄-inch deep soufflé dish with some of the butter, then line the dish with the bread crumbs (see page 8). Attach a soufflé collar that stands 3 inches higher than the top of the dish (see page 8).

2 Melt the remaining butter in a pan, stir in the flour, and cook for 1 minute. Gradually mix in the milk and bring to a boil, stirring until thickened and smooth.

3 Remove the pan from the heat and stir in the crème fraîche or sour cream, dill, lemon zest, egg yolks, and some salt and pepper. Cover and let cool.

4 Beat the egg whites into stiff, moist-looking peaks. Fold the strips of smoked salmon into the cooled sauce, then a large spoonful of egg whites to loosen the mixture. Gently fold in the remaining egg whites.

5 Pour the mixture into the prepared soufflé dish so that it is three-quarters full. Bake in a preheated oven, 375°F, for 30–35 minutes until the soufflé is well risen, the top is browned, and there is a slight wobble to the center.

6 Quickly snip the string off the soufflé collar and gently peel away the paper. Spoon the soufflé onto plates. Serve with extra slices of smoked salmon, if using, and lemon wedges.

roasted bell pepper and rosemary soufflé

1 red bell pepper, cored, seeded, and
   cut into 8 pieces
1 orange bell pepper, cored, seeded,
   and cut into 8 pieces
2 garlic cloves, finely chopped
2 tablespoons olive oil
1 tablespoon balsamic vinegar
5 tablespoons butter
2 tablespoons ready-grated Parmesan
   cheese
1/2 cup all-purpose flour
1 1/3 cups milk
2 tablespoons chopped rosemary
1 cup grated provolone, Gruyère, or
   sharp cheddar cheese
4 eggs, separated
salt and freshly ground black pepper
dressed arugula salad, to serve

Serves 4
Preparation time: 30 minutes
Cooking time: 38–45 minutes

Packed with colorful strips of roasted red and orange bell pepper and flavored with rosemary and garlic, this Mediterranean-inspired soufflé makes a great weekend lunch dish to follow a bowl of steaming soup in winter or a light summer salad.

1 Put the pieces of bell pepper, skin side uppermost, in the bottom of a broiler pan, sprinkle with the chopped garlic, and drizzle with the oil. Broil for 8–10 minutes until the skins are blackened and the bell peppers softened. Turn the bell peppers over, then drizzle with the vinegar, cover with foil, and let cool.

2 Meanwhile, grease a medium tall 6-inch diameter x 3 3/4-inch deep soufflé dish with some of the butter, then line the dish with the Parmesan (see page 8). Attach a soufflé collar that stands 3 inches higher than the top of the dish (see page 8).

3 Melt the remaining butter in a pan, stir in the flour, and cook for 1 minute. Gradually mix in the milk and bring to a boil, stirring until thickened and smooth.

4 Remove the pan from the heat and stir in the rosemary and grated cheese. Beat in the egg yolks and some salt and pepper. Cover and let cool.

5 Peel the skins off the bell peppers using a small, sharp knife, thinly slice the flesh, then stir into the cooled sauce. Beat the egg whites into stiff, moist-looking peaks. Fold a large spoonful into the bell pepper mixture to loosen it, then gently fold in the remaining egg whites.

6 Spoon the mixture into the prepared soufflé dish and bake in a preheated oven, 375°F, for 25–30 minutes until the soufflé is well risen, the top is browned, and there is a slight wobble to the center.

7 Quickly snip the string off the soufflé collar and gently peel away the paper. Spoon the soufflé onto plates. Serve with a dressed arugula salad.

stilton soufflé with arugula

5 tablespoons butter

3 tablespoons fresh bread crumbs

1/2 cup all-purpose flour

1 1/3 cups milk

1 1/4 cups crumbled Stilton cheese

4 eggs, separated

1/2 cup wild arugula leaves, torn into
    pieces, plus extra to serve

salt and freshly ground black pepper

balsamic vinegar, to serve

Serves 4

Preparation time: 30 minutes

Cooking time: 35–40 minutes

Creamy blue cheese complements the peppery taste of arugula beautifully in this tasty soufflé. Watercress or sorrel could be used instead of the arugula leaves.

1 Grease a medium tall 6-inch diameter x 3³/4-inch deep soufflé dish with some of the butter, then line the dish with the bread crumbs (see page 8). Attach a soufflé collar that stands 3 inches higher than the top of the dish (see page 8).

2 Melt the remaining butter in a pan, stir in the flour, and cook for 1 minute. Gradually mix in the milk and bring to a boil, stirring until thickened and smooth.

3 Stir in the cheese until melted, then remove from the heat and stir in the egg yolks and some salt and pepper. Cover and let cool.

4 Beat the egg whites into stiff, moist-looking peaks. Fold the arugula leaves into the cooled sauce, then a large spoonful of egg whites to loosen the mixture. Gently fold in the remaining egg whites.

5 Pour the mixture into the prepared soufflé dish and bake in a preheated oven, 375°F, for 30–35 minutes until the soufflé is well risen, the top is browned, and there is a slight wobble to the center.

6 Quickly snip the string off the soufflé collar and gently peel away the paper. Spoon the soufflé onto plates. Serve with extra arugula leaves dressed with balsamic vinegar.

black olive and basil soufflés

5 tablespoons butter
1/2 cup freshly grated Parmesan
   cheese
1/2 cup all-purpose flour
1 1/3 cups milk
4 eggs, separated
1/4 cup pitted black olives, sliced
4 tablespoons chopped basil
salt and freshly ground black pepper
roasted cherry tomatoes, to serve

Serves 4
Preparation time: 30 minutes
Cooking time: 20–25 minutes

1 Grease 4 small 4-inch diameter x 2 1/2-inch deep soufflé dishes with some of the
butter, then line the dishes with 3 tablespoons of the Parmesan (see page 8).

2 Melt the remaining butter in a pan, stir in the flour, and cook for 1 minute.
Gradually mix in the milk and bring to a boil, stirring until thickened and smooth.

3 Remove the pan from the heat and stir in the remaining Parmesan and the egg
yolks, then the olives and some salt and pepper. Cover and let cool.

4 Beat the egg whites into stiff, moist-looking peaks. Fold a large spoonful into
the cooled sauce, along with the chopped basil, to loosen the mixture, then
gently fold in the remaining egg whites.

5 Pour the mixture into the prepared soufflé dishes and bake in a preheated oven,
375°F, for 15–20 minutes until the soufflés are well risen, the tops are browned,
and there is a slight wobble to the centers. Serve immediately with roasted
cherry tomatoes.

spinach and pine nut soufflés

5 tablespoons butter

3 tablespoons ready-grated Parmesan
cheese

1¹/2 cups frozen leaf spinach,
defrosted

1/2 cup all-purpose flour

1¹/3 cups milk

1/2 cup cream cheese

1 garlic clove, finely crushed

large pinch of grated nutmeg

4 egg yolks

1/3 cup pine nuts

5 egg whites

salt and freshly ground black pepper

Serves 4
Preparation time: 30 minutes
Cooking time: 25 minutes

Forget about tedious rinsing and picking over of spinach leaves, this vibrant green-speckled soufflé is made with labor-saving frozen spinach and flavored with pine nuts and just a hint of garlic and nutmeg.

1 Grease 4 small 4-inch diameter x 2¹/2-inch deep soufflé dishes with some of the butter, then line the dishes with the Parmesan (see page 8). Attach a soufflé collar to each dish that stands 2¹/2 inches higher than the top of the dish (see page 8). Stand the dishes on a baking sheet. Put the spinach in a strainer set over a bowl and press out any water using the back of a spoon.

2 Melt the remaining butter in a pan, stir in the flour, and cook for 1 minute. Gradually mix in the milk and bring to a boil, stirring until thickened and smooth.

3 Remove the pan from the heat and stir in the cream cheese, garlic, and nutmeg. Mix in the egg yolks, spinach, half the pine nuts, and some salt and pepper. Cover and let cool.

4 Beat the egg whites into stiff, moist-looking peaks. Fold a large spoonful into the cooled sauce to loosen the mixture, then gently fold in the remaining egg whites.

5 Spoon the mixture into the prepared soufflé dishes, then sprinkle with the remaining pine nuts. Bake in a preheated oven, 375°F, for 20 minutes until the soufflés are well risen, their tops are browned, and there is a slight wobble to the centers. Quickly snip the string off the soufflé collars and gently peel away the paper. Serve immediately.

fine herb, ricotta, and shallot soufflé

5 tablespoons butter
3 tablespoons fresh bread crumbs
1 tablespoon olive oil
1/2 cup finely chopped shallots
1/2 cup all-purpose flour
1 1/3 cups milk
1/2 cup ricotta cheese
4 egg yolks
5 egg whites
2 tablespoons chopped mixed herbs, to
   include rosemary, sage, and thyme
4 tablespoons chopped parsley or
   chives
salt and freshly ground black pepper
roasted cherry tomatoes, to serve

Serves 4
Preparation time: 30 minutes
Cooking time: 35–40 minutes

1 Grease a medium tall 6-inch diameter x 3³/₄-inch deep soufflé dish with some of the butter, then line the dish with the bread crumbs (see page 8). Attach a soufflé collar that stands 3 inches higher than the top of the dish (see page 8).

2 Heat the oil in a skillet, add the shallots, and fry gently for 5 minutes, stirring frequently, until softened and just beginning to turn golden.

3 Meanwhile, melt the remaining butter in a pan, stir in the flour, and cook for 1 minute. Gradually mix in the milk and bring to a boil, stirring until thickened and smooth.

4 Remove the pan from the heat and stir in the ricotta cheese, egg yolks, cooked shallots, and some salt and pepper. Cover and let cool.

5 Beat the egg whites into stiff, moist-looking peaks. Add the chopped herbs to the cooled sauce, then fold in a large spoonful of egg whites to loosen the mixture. Gently fold in the remaining egg whites.

6 Pour the mixture into the prepared soufflé dish and bake in a preheated oven, 375°F, for 25–30 minutes until the soufflé is well risen, the top is browned, and there is a slight wobble to the center.

7 Quickly snip the string off the soufflé collar and gently peel away the paper. Spoon the soufflé onto plates. Serve with roasted cherry tomatoes.

fruits de mer soufflé

5 tablespoons butter

2 tablespoons ready-grated Parmesan
   cheese

1/2 cup all-purpose flour

1 1/3 cups milk

grated zest of 1 lemon

4 eggs, separated

8 oz mixed cooked seafood, defrosted
   if frozen, rinsed with cold water, and
   very coarsely chopped

4 tablespoons chopped chives

salt and freshly ground black pepper

To serve

watercress salad

warm crusty bread

lemon wedges

Serves 4

Preparation time: 30 minutes

Cooking time: 35–40 minutes

This gourmet-style seafood soufflé is packed with chunky pieces of shrimp, mussel, and squid and flavored with chopped chives and lemon. It makes a delightful light supper dish served with a crisp watercress salad and warm crusty bread.

1 Grease a medium tall 6-inch diameter x 3³/4-inch deep soufflé dish with some of the butter, then line the dish with the Parmesan (see page 8). Attach a soufflé collar that stands 3 inches higher than the top of the dish (see page 8).

2 Melt the remaining butter in a pan, stir in the flour, and cook for 1 minute. Gradually mix in the milk and bring to a boil, stirring until thickened and smooth.

3 Remove the pan from the heat and stir in the lemon zest, egg yolks, and some salt and pepper. Cover and let cool.

4 Beat the egg whites into stiff, moist-looking peaks. Fold a large spoonful into the cooled sauce to loosen the mixture, then fold in the seafood and chives. Gently fold in the remaining egg whites.

5 Spoon the mixture into the prepared soufflé dish and bake in a preheated oven, 375°F, for 30–35 minutes until the soufflé is well risen, the top is browned, and there is a slight wobble to the center.

6 Quickly snip the string off the soufflé collar and gently peel away the paper. Spoon the soufflé onto plates. Serve with a watercress salad, warm crusty bread, and lemon wedges.

sautéed fennel and parma ham soufflés

5 tablespoons butter

3 tablespoons fresh bread crumbs

7 oz fennel bulb

1 tablespoon olive oil

1/2 cup all-purpose flour

11/3 cups milk

4 eggs, separated

3 oz sliced Parma ham, cut into
    pieces

salt and freshly ground black pepper

Serves 4

Preparation time: 30 minutes

Cooking time: 25–30 minutes

Fennel is one of those vegetables that is seldom used and yet its delicate aniseed flavor goes well with milky sauces or creamy dishes. It is generally sold trimmed, but if there are a lot of green feathery tops still in place, then chop these and use 2 tablespoons in the soufflé.

1 Grease 4 small 4-inch diameter x 2¹/₂-inch deep soufflé dishes with some of the butter, then line the dishes with the bread crumbs (see page 8). Stand the dishes on a baking sheet.

2 Halve the fennel, cut out the woody core, and discard. Reserve any green feathery tops and finely chop the remaining fennel. Heat the oil in a skillet, add the chopped fennel, and fry gently for 5 minutes, stirring occasionally, until softened. Chop and add any green tops.

3 Meanwhile, melt the remaining butter in a pan, stir in the flour, and cook for 1 minute. Gradually mix in the milk and bring to a boil, stirring until thickened and smooth.

4 Remove the pan from the heat and stir in the egg yolks, then the sautéed fennel and some salt and pepper. Cover and let cool.

5 Beat the egg whites into stiff, moist-looking peaks. Fold a large spoonful into the cooled sauce to loosen the mixture, then fold in the pieces of Parma ham. Gently fold in the remaining egg whites.

6 Pour the mixture into the prepared soufflé dishes and bake in a preheated oven, 375°F, for 15–20 minutes until the soufflés are well risen, their tops are browned, and there is a slight wobble to the centers. Serve immediately.

hot peppered chorizo soufflés

5 tablespoons butter
3 tablespoons fresh bread crumbs
1/2 cup all-purpose flour
1 1/3 cups milk
1 cup grated manchego or cheddar
   cheese
1/2–1 teaspoon ready-chopped red chili
4 eggs, separated
2 oz sliced cured chorizo sausage,
   skinned and diced
salt and freshly ground black pepper
green salad, to serve

Serves 4
Preparation time: 30 minutes
Cooking time: 20–25 minutes

1 Grease 4 small 4-inch diameter x 2 1/2-inch deep soufflé dishes with some of
the butter, then line the dishes with the bread crumbs (see page 8). Stand the
dishes on a baking sheet.

2 Melt the remaining butter in a pan, stir in the flour, and cook for 1 minute.
Gradually mix in the milk and bring to a boil, stirring until thickened and smooth.

3 Remove the pan from the heat and stir in the cheese, chili to taste, egg yolks,
and some salt and pepper. Cover and let cool.

4 Beat the egg whites into stiff, moist-looking peaks. Fold the diced chorizo
sausage into the cooled sauce, then a large spoonful of egg whites to loosen
the mixture. Gently fold in the remaining egg whites.

5 Spoon the mixture into the prepared soufflé dishes and bake in a preheated
oven, 375°F, for 15–20 minutes until the soufflés are well risen, their tops are
browned, and there is a slight wobble to the centers. Serve immediately with a
crisp green salad.

hot and chilled sweet soufflés

white choc soufflés with dark chocolate sauce

butter, for greasing

1/3 cup superfine sugar, plus
    4 teaspoons for lining the dishes

3 egg yolks

1/3 cup all-purpose flour

1 cup milk

6 oz white chocolate,
    coarsely chopped

1 teaspoon vanilla extract

5 egg whites

sifted drinking chocolate powder and
    confectioners' sugar, for dusting

Chocolate sauce

5 oz bittersweet chocolate, broken
    into pieces

1/2 cup milk

4 tablespoons heavy cream

1 tablespoon superfine sugar

Serves 4
Preparation time: 30 minutes
Cooking time: 15–17 minutes

For chocoholics, these light, fluffy soufflés will prove to be a winner! Dotted with just-melted chunks of white chocolate, they are served with a glossy, rich, velvety, dark chocolate sauce enriched with heavy cream.

1 Lightly butter 4 small 4-inch diameter x $2^1/2$-inch deep soufflé dishes, then line each dish with 1 teaspoon superfine sugar (see page 8). Stand the dishes on a baking sheet.

2 Beat half the remaining superfine sugar and the egg yolks in a bowl until thick, pale, and mousse-like. Sift the flour over the surface, then gently fold it in.

3 Bring the milk just to a boil in a pan, then gradually beat it into the egg yolk mixture. Return the milk mixture to the pan and cook over medium heat, stirring continuously until thickened and smooth. Remove the pan from the heat, add half the white chocolate, and stir until melted. Mix in the vanilla extract, cover, and let cool.

4 Beat the egg whites into stiff, moist-looking peaks. Gradually beat in the remaining superfine sugar, a teaspoon at a time, until thick and glossy. Fold a large spoonful of egg whites into the cooled sauce to loosen the mixture, then fold in the remaining white chocolate. Gently fold in the remaining egg whites.

5 Spoon the mixture into the prepared soufflé dishes and bake in a preheated oven, 425°F, for 10–12 minutes until the soufflés are well risen, their tops are browned, and there is a slight wobble to the centers.

6 Meanwhile, gently heat all the sauce ingredients together in a small pan, stirring until smooth, then pour into a serving pitcher. Dust the tops of the soufflés with sifted drinking chocolate powder and confectioners' sugar and serve immediately, with some of the warmed sauce drizzled over each one.

dark chocolate soufflé with crème anglaise

butter, for greasing

1/2 cup superfine sugar, plus
    1 tablespoon for lining the dish

3 egg yolks

1/3 cup all-purpose flour

1 cup milk

4 oz bittersweet chocolate, broken
    into pieces

5 egg whites

sifted drinking chocolate powder and
    confectioners' sugar, for dusting

Crème anglaise

2 egg yolks

2 tablespoons superfine sugar

1 teaspoon cornstarch

1 cup milk

2 tablespoons heavy cream

1/2 teaspoon vanilla extract

Serves 4
Preparation time: 30 minutes
Cooking time: 30–35 minutes

This incredibly rich, bittersweet, dark chocolate soufflé is served with a creamy smooth vanilla custard sauce for an irresistible mealtime finale. You can make the soufflé base and crème anglaise earlier in the day if preferred, but sprinkle the surface of the custard with a little extra sugar or place a piece of wetted parchment paper on it to prevent a skin forming.

1 Lightly butter a medium tall 6-inch diameter x 3³/₄-inch deep soufflé dish, then line the dish with 1 tablespoon superfine sugar (see page 8). Attach a soufflé collar that stands 3 inches higher than the top of the dish (see page 8).

2 Beat half the remaining superfine sugar and the egg yolks in a bowl until thick, pale, and mousse-like. Sift the flour over the surface, then gently fold it in.

3 Bring the milk just to a boil in a pan, then gradually beat it into the egg yolk mixture. Return the milk mixture to the pan and cook over medium heat, stirring continuously until thickened and smooth. Remove from the heat, add the chocolate, and stir until melted. Cover and let cool.

4 Beat the egg whites into stiff, moist-looking peaks. Gradually beat in the remaining superfine sugar, a teaspoon at a time, until thick and glossy. Fold a large spoonful of egg whites into the cooled sauce to loosen the mixture, then gently fold in the remaining egg whites.

5 Spoon the mixture into the prepared soufflé dish and bake in a preheated oven, 400°F, for 25–30 minutes until the soufflé is well risen, the top is browned, and there is a slight wobble to the center.

6 Meanwhile, make the crème anglaise by combining the egg yolks, sugar and cornstarch, as in Step 2. Bring the milk just to a boil in a small pan then gradually add to the egg yolk mixture. Return the milk mixture to the pan and cook over medium heat, stirring continuously until thickened and smooth and the custard coats the back of the spoon. Stir in the cream and vanilla extract and set aside.

7 Quickly snip the string off the soufflé collar and gently peel away the paper. Dust the top of the soufflé with sifted drinking chocolate powder and confectioners' sugar and serve immediately, with the warm custard sauce.

classic grand marnier soufflé

butter, for greasing
1/2 cup superfine sugar, plus
   1 tablespoon for lining the dish
3 egg yolks
1/3 cup all-purpose flour
1 cup milk
4 tablespoons Grand Marnier
grated zest of 2 oranges
5 egg whites
sifted confectioners' sugar, for dusting

Serves 4
Preparation time: 30 minutes
Cooking time: 20–25 minutes

1 Lightly butter a medium tall 6-inch diameter x 3³/4-inch deep soufflé dish, then line the dish with 1 tablespoon superfine sugar (see page 8). Attach a soufflé collar that stands 3 inches higher than the top of the dish (see page 8).

2 Beat half the remaining superfine sugar and the egg yolks in a bowl until thick, pale, and mousse-like. Sift the flour over the surface, then gently fold it in.

3 Bring the milk just to a boil in a pan then gradually beat it into the egg yolk mixture. Return the milk mixture to the pan and cook over medium heat, stirring continuously until thickened and smooth. Remove from the heat and stir in the Grand Marnier and orange zest. Cover and let cool.

4 Beat the egg whites into stiff, moist-looking peaks. Gradually beat in the remaining superfine sugar, a teaspoon at a time, until thick and glossy. Fold a large spoonful of egg whites into the cooled sauce to loosen the mixture, then gently fold in the remaining egg whites.

5 Spoon the mixture into the prepared soufflé dish and bake in a preheated oven, 425°F, for 17–20 minutes until the soufflé is well risen, the top is browned, and there is a slight wobble to the center. Quickly snip the string off the soufflé collar and gently peel away the paper. Dust the top of the soufflé with sifted confectioners' sugar and serve immediately.

creamy lemon soufflés

butter, for greasing
1/2 cup superfine sugar, plus
   4 teaspoons for lining the dishes
3 egg yolks
1/3 cup all-purpose flour
3/4 cup milk
3 tablespoons heavy cream
grated zest of 2 lemons
freshly squeezed juice of 1 lemon,
   strained
5 egg whites
sifted confectioners' sugar, for dusting

Serves 4
Preparation time: 30 minutes
Cooking time: 15–17 minutes

Made with pantry ingredients, these soufflés are ideal for when you want to transform an everyday meal into something extra special.

1 Lightly butter 4 small 4-inch diameter x 2^1/$_2$-inch deep soufflé dishes, then line each dish with 1 teaspoon superfine sugar (see page 8). Stand the dishes on a baking sheet.

2 Beat half the remaining superfine sugar and the egg yolks in a bowl until thick, pale, and mousse-like. Sift the flour over the surface, then gently fold it in.

3 Bring the milk and cream just to a boil in a pan, then gradually beat into the egg yolk mixture. Return the milk mixture to the pan and cook over medium heat, stirring continuously until thickened and smooth. Beat in the lemon zest and juice, then remove from the heat, cover, and let cool.

4 Beat the egg whites into stiff, moist-looking peaks. Gradually beat in the remaining superfine sugar, a teaspoon at a time, until thick and glossy. Fold a large spoonful of egg whites into the cooled sauce to loosen the mixture, then gently fold in the remaining egg whites.

5 Spoon the mixture into the prepared soufflé dishes and bake in a preheated oven, 425°F, for 10–12 minutes until the soufflés are well risen, their tops are browned, and there is a slight wobble to the centers. Dust the tops of the soufflés with sifted confectioners' sugar and serve immediately.

very berry soufflés with red berry coulis

butter, for greasing
1/2 cup superfine sugar, plus
    4 teaspoons for lining the dishes
3 egg yolks
1/3 cup all-purpose flour
1 cup milk
grated zest of 1/2 lemon
5 egg whites
1 cup mixed red berry fruits, defrosted
    if frozen, plus extra to serve
sifted confectioners' sugar, for dusting

Coulis
2 1/2 cups raspberries, defrosted
    if frozen
2 tablespoons superfine sugar

Serves 4
Preparation time: 30 minutes
Cooking time: 15–17 minutes

Dotted with whole berry fruits, this delicate, airy soufflé is served with a speedy puréed fruit sauce, lightly sweetened to taste.

1 Lightly butter 4 small 4-inch diameter x 2 1/2-inch deep glass dishes, then line each dish with 1 teaspoon superfine sugar (see page 8). Stand the dishes on a baking sheet.

2 Beat half the remaining superfine sugar and the egg yolks in a bowl until thick, pale, and mousse-like. Sift the flour over the surface, then gently fold it in.

3 Bring the milk just to a boil in a pan, then gradually beat it into the egg yolk mixture. Return the milk mixture to the pan and cook over medium heat, stirring continuously until thickened and smooth. Stir in the lemon zest, cover, and let cool.

4 Beat the egg whites into stiff, moist-looking peaks. Gradually beat in the remaining superfine sugar, a teaspoon at a time, until thick and glossy. Fold a large spoonful of egg whites into the cooled sauce to loosen the mixture, then gently fold in the remaining egg whites, followed by the mixed berries.

5 Spoon the mixture into the prepared glass dishes and bake in a preheated oven, 425°F, for 10–12 minutes until the soufflés are well risen, their tops are browned, and there is a slight wobble to the centers. Meanwhile, make the coulis by blending the raspberries in a blender or food processor, press through a strainer into a bowl, then stir in the superfine sugar.

6 Dust the tops of the soufflés with sifted confectioners' sugar and serve immediately, with the raspberry coulis and extra mixed berries.

hazelnut soufflés

butter, for greasing

2 tablespoons ground almonds

1/4 cup superfine sugar

1/4 cup brown sugar

3 egg yolks

1/3 cup all-purpose flour

1 cup milk

1/3 cup hazelnuts, plus extra coarsely
   chopped, to decorate

5 egg whites

sifted confectioners' sugar, for dusting

Serves 4

Preparation time: 30 minutes

Cooking time: 15–17 minutes

Hazelnuts are much less frequently used than other nuts, yet they have a stronger, more mellow taste, especially when toasted first. These soufflés are delicious served with crème anglaise or chocolate sauce (see page 34 or 32).

1 Lightly butter 4 small 4-inch diameter x 2^1/$_2$-inch deep soufflé dishes, then line each dish with ^{1}/$_2$ tablespoon ground almonds (see page 8). Stand the dishes on a baking sheet.

2 Mix the sugars together, then beat half in a bowl with the egg yolks until thick, pale, and mousse-like. Sift the flour over the surface, then gently fold it in.

3 Bring the milk just to a boil in a pan, then gradually beat it into the egg yolk mixture. Return the milk mixture to the pan and cook over medium heat, stirring continuously until thickened and smooth.

4 Place the whole hazelnuts on a piece of foil and toast under the broiler until lightly browned. Finely chop, then stir into the sauce. Cover and let cool.

5 Beat the egg whites into stiff, moist-looking peaks. Gradually beat in the remaining sugar, a teaspoon at a time, until thick and glossy. Fold a large spoonful of egg whites into the cooled sauce to loosen the mixture, then gently fold in the remaining egg whites.

6 Spoon the mixture into the prepared soufflé dishes, sprinkle with the coarsely chopped hazelnuts, and bake in a preheated oven, 425°F, for 10–12 minutes until the soufflés are well risen, their tops are browned, and there is a slight wobble to the centers. Dust the tops of the soufflés liberally with sifted confectioners' sugar and serve immediately.

apple soufflé with cinnamon cream

butter, for greasing
1 tablespoon ground almonds
1 cooking apple, about 9 oz, quartered,
    cored, peeled, and thinly sliced
1 tablespoon water
1/4 cup superfine sugar
1/4 cup brown sugar
3 egg yolks
1/3 cup all-purpose flour
1 cup milk
1/8 teaspoon ground cinnamon
5 egg whites
sifted confectioners' sugar, for dusting

Cinnamon cream sauce
1 cup heavy cream
2 teaspoons brown sugar
2 large pinches of ground cinnamon

Serves 4
Preparation time: 30 minutes
Cooking time: 30 minutes

This light, delicate, fruit-flavored soufflé is made with tart cooking apples and complemented by a smooth, creamy sauce that can be stirred together in a matter of seconds.

1 Lightly butter a medium tall 6-inch diameter x 3³/4-inch deep soufflé dish, then line the dish with the ground almonds (see page 8). Attach a soufflé collar that stands 3 inches higher than the top of the dish (see page 8).

2 Place the apple slices in a small pan with the water. Cover and cook gently for 5 minutes or until pulpy.

3 Mix the sugars together, then beat half in a bowl with the egg yolks until thick, pale, and mousse-like. Sift the flour over the surface, then gently fold it in.

4 Bring the milk just to a boil in a pan, then gradually beat it into the egg yolk mixture. Return the milk mixture to the pan and cook over medium heat, stirring continuously until thickened and smooth. Stir in the cooked apple and the ground cinnamon, cover, and let cool.

5 Beat the egg whites into stiff, moist-looking peaks. Gradually beat in the remaining sugar, a teaspoon at a time, until thick and glossy. Fold a large spoonful of egg whites into the cooled sauce to loosen the mixture, then gently fold in the remaining egg whites.

6 Spoon the mixture into the prepared soufflé dish, and bake in a preheated oven, 425°F, for about 20 minutes until the soufflé is well risen, the top is browned, and there is a slight wobble to the center. Meanwhile, stir the sauce ingredients together and gently warm, if desired.

7 When cooked, dust the top of the soufflé with sifted confectioners' sugar, snip the string off the soufflé collar, and gently peel away the paper. Spoon the soufflé into dishes and serve immediately with the cream sauce drizzled over.

cranberry and orange soufflés

butter, for greasing
1/2 cup superfine sugar, plus
  4 teaspoons for lining the dishes
1/2 cup dried cranberries
grated zest of 2 oranges
3 tablespoons freshly squeezed
  orange juice
3 egg yolks
1/3 cup all-purpose flour
1 cup milk
5 egg whites
sifted confectioners' sugar, for dusting
orange zest curls, to decorate (see
  page 57)

Serves 4
Preparation time: 30 minutes, plus
  standing
Cooking time: 15–17 minutes

Serve these soufflés with cream or crème fraîche flavored with a little Cointreau, if desired. Use 1/2 cup fresh cranberries instead of the dried fruit, if preferred—cook them with the orange zest, juice, and 2 tablespoons water until the berries have softened. Let cool, then fold into the cooled sauce at Step 5, as below.

1 Lightly butter 4 small 4-inch diameter x 2^1/2-inch deep soufflé dishes, then line each dish with 1 teaspoon superfine sugar (see page 8). Stand the dishes on a baking sheet.

2 Warm the dried cranberries, orange zest, and juice together in a small pan. Remove from the heat and leave the cranberries to plump up for about 30 minutes.

3 Beat half the remaining superfine sugar and the egg yolks in a bowl until thick, pale, and mousse-like. Sift the flour over the surface, then gently fold it in.

4 Bring the milk just to a boil in a pan, then gradually beat it into the egg yolk mixture. Return the milk mixture to the pan and cook over medium heat, stirring continuously until thickened and smooth. Cover and let cool.

5 Beat the egg whites into stiff, moist-looking peaks. Gradually beat in the remaining superfine sugar, a teaspoon at a time, until thick and glossy. Fold a large spoonful of egg whites into the cooled sauce to loosen the mixture, then mix in the soaked cranberries. Gently fold in the remaining egg whites.

6 Spoon the mixture into the prepared soufflé dishes and bake in a preheated oven, 425°F, for 10–12 minutes until the soufflés are well risen, their tops are browned, and there is a slight wobble to the centers. Dust the tops of the soufflés with confectioners' sugar and decorate with orange zest curls. Serve immediately.

twice-baked cappuccino soufflés

butter, for greasing
3 egg yolks
1/3 cup golden superfine sugar
1/3 cup all-purpose flour
1 cup milk
2 teaspoons instant coffee granules
   or powder
2 egg whites

To finish
1 cup heavy cream
3 tablespoons golden superfine sugar
1 teaspoon instant coffee granules or
   powder
2 tablespoons brandy or whiskey
   (optional)
3 oz bittersweet chocolate, broken into
   pieces
sifted drinking chocolate powder,
   for dusting

Serves 6
Preparation time: 30 minutes
Cooking time: 20 minutes, plus cooling
Reheating time: 12–15 minutes

Reminiscent of a light coffee custard, these double-baked soufflés are first baked in soufflé dishes, then turned out, drizzled with cream, and reheated before being served with a creamy coffee sauce and dusted with drinking chocolate powder for an authentic cappuccino finish.

1 Lightly butter 6 individual 3-inch diameter x 1 1/2-inch deep soufflé dishes, then stand them on a rack in a roasting pan.

2 Beat the egg yolks and superfine sugar in a bowl until thick, pale, and mousse-like. Sift the flour over the surface, then gently fold it in.

3 Bring the milk just to a boil in a pan, then gradually beat it into the egg yolk mixture. Return the milk mixture to the pan and cook over medium heat, stirring continuously until thickened and smooth. Stir in the instant coffee until dissolved. Cover and let cool for 15 minutes.

4 Beat the egg whites into stiff, moist-looking peaks. Fold a large spoonful into the cooled sauce to loosen the mixture, then fold in the remaining egg whites.

5 Spoon the mixture into the prepared soufflé dishes and pour hot water into the roasting pan to come halfway up the sides of the dishes. Bake, uncovered, in a preheated oven, 350°F, for 15 minutes until the soufflés are well risen and spongy to the touch. Lift the dishes out of the pan and let cool slightly. Then run a knife around the edges and unmold the soufflés, with the tops uppermost, into a buttered shallow ovenproof dish, leaving a little room between them.

6 When ready to reheat, drizzle 1 tablespoon cream over each soufflé and sprinkle each one with 1/2 teaspoon of the sugar. Bake, uncovered, in a preheated oven, 350°F for 12–15 minutes until hot and slightly puffed up.

7 Meanwhile, warm the remaining cream and the remaining sugar in a small pan until the sugar has dissolved. Stir in the coffee and brandy or whiskey, if using. Melt the chocolate in a bowl over hot water, then spoon into a paper piping bag and snip off the tip. Pipe squiggly lines around the edges of 6 serving plates.

8 Drizzle the coffee sauce inside the chocolate line on each plate. Add the reheated soufflés, quickly dust with drinking chocolate, and serve immediately.

individual lemon and vodka soufflés

4 tablespoons cold water

4 teaspoons powdered gelatin

4 eggs, separated

3/4 cup superfine sugar

finely grated zest of 2 1/2 lemons

2/3 cup strained freshly squeezed
lemon juice

4 tablespoons vodka

1 cup heavy cream

To decorate

1/2 cup heavy cream, whipped

lemon zest curls (see page 57)

coarsely chopped pistachio nuts

Serves 6

Preparation time: 30 minutes, plus
chilling

Cooking time: 13–14 minutes

If you don't have any individual soufflé dishes, you can serve these soufflés in tall wine glasses instead. Serve the soufflés soon after decorating, leaving the paper collars on until the last minute.

1 Attach soufflé collars to 6 individual 3-inch diameter x 1 1/2-inch deep soufflé dishes so that the paper stands 1 1/2 inches higher than the top of each dish (see page 8). Stand the dishes on a tray.

2 Put the water in a small heatproof bowl or mug and sprinkle over the gelatin, making sure that the water absorbs all the powder. Set aside for 5 minutes, then stand the bowl in a small pan half-filled with boiling water and simmer for 3–4 minutes, stirring occasionally, until the gelatin dissolves to a clear liquid.

3 Put the egg yolks, sugar, and lemon zest in a large heatproof bowl, then stand the bowl over a pan of simmering water so that the bottom of the bowl is not touching the water. Beat using a hand-held electric beater for about 10 minutes until the eggs are very thick and pale, and the beater leaves a trail when lifted above the mixture.

4 Gradually beat in the strained lemon juice and continue beating until thick once more. Remove the bowl from the heat and continue beating until cool.

5 Gradually fold in the dissolved gelatin, adding it in a thin, steady stream, then fold in the vodka.

6 Softly whip the cream (no need to wash the beaters in between), then fold into the soufflé mixture. Chill if the mixture is very soft.

7 Wash the beaters and dry well, then use to beat the egg whites into stiff, moist-looking peaks. Fold a large spoonful into the soufflé mixture to loosen it, then gently fold in the remaining egg whites. Pour the mixture into the prepared soufflé dishes so that it stands above the rim of the dishes. Chill for 4 hours or until set.

8 To serve, snip the string off the soufflé collars and gently peel away the paper. Add a spoonful of whipped cream to the center of each soufflé and top with lemon zest curls and a few chopped pistachio nuts. Return to the refrigerator and serve within 30 minutes.

marbled blueberry and white chocolate soufflés

4 tablespoons water

4 teaspoons powdered gelatin

4 eggs, separated

2/3 cup superfine sugar

1 cup heavy cream

2 cups blueberries, defrosted if frozen, puréed, and pressed through a strainer

4 oz white chocolate, melted

Serves 6

Preparation time: 40 minutes, plus chilling

Cooking time: 13–14 minutes

1 Attach soufflé collars to 6 individual 3-inch diameter x 1¹/₂-inch deep glass dishes so that the paper stands 1¹/₂ inches higher than the top of each dish (see page 8). Stand the dishes on a tray.

2 Put the water in a small heatproof bowl or mug and sprinkle over the gelatin, making sure that the water absorbs all the powder. Set aside for 5 minutes, then stand the bowl in a small pan half-filled with boiling water and simmer for 3–4 minutes, stirring occasionally, until the gelatin dissolves to a clear liquid.

3 Put the egg yolks and sugar in a large heatproof bowl, then stand the bowl over a pan of simmering water so that the bottom of the bowl is not touching the water. Beat using a hand held electric beater for about 10 minutes until the eggs are very thick and pale, and the beater leaves a trail when lifted above the mixture. Remove the bowl from the heat and continue beating until cool.

4 Gradually fold in the dissolved gelatin, adding it in a thin, steady stream. Softly whip the cream (no need to wash the beaters in between), then fold into the soufflé mixture.

5 Spoon one-third of the mixture into a separate bowl and fold in the strained blueberry purée. Fold the melted chocolate into the remaining mixture in the original bowl.

6 Wash the beaters and dry well, then use to beat the egg whites into stiff, moist-looking peaks. Fold a spoonful into each bowl of chocolate and blueberry soufflé mixture to loosen, then gently fold in the remaining egg whites, adding one-third to the blueberry mixture and the rest to the chocolate mixture.

7 Add alternate spoonfuls of each soufflé mixture to the prepared glass dishes so that they stand above the rim of the dishes. Run a knife through the mixtures to create a marbled effect, then chill for 4 hours or overnight until set. To serve, snip the string off the soufflé collars and gently peel away the paper.

chilled blackcurrant and mint soufflé

1¹/2 cups blackcurrants, defrosted
   if frozen

6 tablespoons water

4 teaspoons powdered gelatin

4 eggs, separated

1 cup superfine sugar

1 cup heavy cream

5 tablespoons finely chopped mint

4 teaspoons sifted confectioners'
   sugar, for dusting

Serves 6

Preparation time: 40 minutes, plus
   chilling

Cooking time: 18–19 minutes

1 Attach a soufflé collar to a small 5¹/2-inch diameter x 2¹/2-inch deep soufflé dish so that the paper stands 2¹/2 inches higher than the top of the dish (see page 8).

2 Put the blackcurrants in a small pan with 2 tablespoons of the water, cover, and cook gently for 5 minutes until softened. Blend in a blender or food processor until smooth, then press through a strainer.

3 Meanwhile, put the remaining water in a small heatproof bowl or mug and sprinkle over the gelatin, making sure that the water absorbs all the powder. Set aside for 5 minutes, then stand the bowl in a small pan half-filled with boiling water and simmer for 3–4 minutes, stirring occasionally, until the gelatin dissolves to a clear liquid.

4 Put the egg yolks and superfine sugar in a heatproof large bowl, then stand the bowl over a pan of simmering water so that the bottom of the bowl is not touching the water. Beat using a hand-held electric beater for about 10 minutes until the eggs are very thick and pale, and the beater leaves a trail when lifted above the mixture. Remove the bowl from the heat and continue beating until cool.

5 Gradually fold in the dissolved gelatin, adding it in a thin, steady stream, then fold in the blackcurrant purée.

6 Softly whip the cream (no need to wash the beaters in between), then fold into the soufflé mixture with the chopped mint.

7 Wash the beater and dry well, then use to beat the egg whites into stiff, moist-looking peaks. Fold a large spoonful into the soufflé mixture to loosen it, then gently fold in the remaining egg whites. Pour the mixture into the prepared soufflé dish so that it stands above the rim of the dish. Chill for 4 hours or until set.

8 To serve, snip the string off the soufflé collar and gently peel away the paper. Arrange 4 or 5 curved strips of nonstick parchment paper about 1 inch wide over the soufflé top so that some overlap, then dust with sifted confectioners' sugar. Carefully lift off the paper strips and serve immediately or the sugar will dissolve and disappear.

strawberry and lavender soufflés

3 cups fresh strawberries, hulled

4 tablespoons water

4 teaspoons powdered gelatin

4 eggs, separated

2/3 cup superfine sugar

4–5 lavender sprigs, petals crumbled, stems discarded

1 cup heavy cream

a few drops of pink or red food coloring (optional)

small bunch of lavender, to decorate

Serves 6

Preparation time: 40 minutes, plus chilling

Cooking time: 13–14 minutes

Subtly flavored with just a hint of fresh lavender, these delicate strawberry soufflés seem to encapsulate the very essence of summer.

1 Attach soufflé collars to 6 individual 3-inch diameter x 1 1/2-inch deep soufflé dishes so that the paper stands 1 1/2 inches higher than the top of each dish (see page 8). Stand the dishes on a tray.

2 Slice 6 strawberries and divide them between the bottoms of the soufflé dishes. Blend the remaining strawberries to a coarse purée in a blender or food processor, or use a potato masher.

3 Put the water in a small heatproof bowl or mug and sprinkle over the gelatin, making sure that the water absorbs all the powder. Set aside for 5 minutes, then stand the bowl in a small pan half-filled with boiling water and simmer for 3–4 minutes, stirring occasionally, until the gelatin dissolves to a clear liquid.

4 Put the egg yolks, sugar, and lavender petals in a large heatproof bowl, then stand the bowl over a pan of simmering water so that the bottom of the bowl is not touching the water. Beat using a hand-held electric beater for about 10 minutes until the eggs are very thick and pale, and the beater leaves a trail when lifted above the mixture. Remove the bowl from the heat and continue beating until cool.

5 Gradually fold in the dissolved gelatin, adding it in a thin, steady stream, then fold in the strawberry purée.

6 Softly whip the cream (no need to wash the beaters in between), then fold into the soufflé mixture with the food coloring, if using. Chill if the mixture is very soft.

7 Wash the beaters and dry well, then use to beat the egg whites into stiff, moist-looking peaks. Fold a large spoonful into the soufflé mixture to loosen it, then gently fold in the remaining egg whites. Pour the mixture into the prepared soufflé dishes so that it stands above the rim of the dishes. Chill for 4 hours or until set.

8 To serve, peel back the paper collars and tuck a few trimmed lavender stems under the string.

passion fruit and lime soufflé

4 tablespoons water
4 teaspoons powdered gelatin
4 eggs, separated
3/4 cup superfine sugar
grated zest of 3 limes
5 tablespoons freshly squeezed
   lime juice
8 passion fruit, halved
1 cup heavy cream

Serves 6
Preparation time: 40 minutes, plus
   chilling
Cooking time: 13–14 minutes

Passion fruit add the most wonderful exotic perfume and intense flavor to this light, frothy, lime soufflé. It is not true that the wrinklier they are the better, they are simply older fruits.

1 Attach a soufflé collar to a small 5^1/$_2$-inch diameter x 2^1/$_2$-inch deep soufflé dish so that the paper stands 2^1/$_2$ inches higher than the top of the dish (see page 8).

2 Put the water in a small heatproof bowl or mug and sprinkle over the gelatin, making sure that the water absorbs all the powder. Set aside for 5 minutes, then stand the bowl in a small pan half-filled with boiling water and simmer for 3–4 minutes, stirring occasionally, until the gelatin dissolves to a clear liquid.

3 Put the egg yolks, sugar, and lime zest in a large heatproof bowl, then stand the bowl over a pan of simmering water so that the bottom of the bowl is not touching the water. Beat using a hand-held electric beater for about 10 minutes until the eggs are very thick and pale, and the beater leaves a trail when lifted above the mixture.

4 Gradually beat in the lime juice and beat until thick once more. Remove the bowl from the heat and continue beating until cool.

5 Gradually fold in the dissolved gelatin, adding it in a thin, steady stream. Scoop the seeds out of 6 of the passion fruit and fold into the soufflé mixture.

6 Softly whip the cream (no need to wash the beaters in between), then fold into the soufflé mixture and chill for 20–30 minutes until just beginning to set. Lightly stir the mixture once more to redistribute any passion fruit seeds that may have sunk to the bottom.

7 Wash the beaters and dry well, then use to beat the egg whites into stiff, moist-looking peaks. Fold a large spoonful into the soufflé mixture to loosen it, then gently fold in the remaining egg whites. Pour the mixture into the prepared soufflé dish so that it stands above the rim of the dish. Chill for 4 hours or until set.

8 To serve, snip the string off the soufflé collar and gently peel away the paper. Top the soufflé with seeds scooped from the remaining 2 passion fruit.

healthy soufflés

spicy sweet potato soufflé

1 small sweet potato, about 7 oz, peeled and finely diced

2 tablespoons olive oil, plus extra for greasing

2 tablespoons fresh bread crumbs

2 tablespoons butter

1 teaspoon cumin seeds, coarsely crushed

1 teaspoon fennel seeds, coarsely crushed

1 garlic clove, crushed

1/2 cup all-purpose flour

1 1/3 cups skim milk

4 eggs, separated

1/2 teaspoon turmeric

1/2 teaspoon paprika

salt and freshly ground black pepper

Serves 4
Preparation time: 30 minutes
Cooking time: 35–40 minutes

The orange color of this eye-catching soufflé is achieved by mixing sweet potato with vibrant yellow turmeric, deep red paprika, and fennel and cumin seeds crushed using a mortar and pestle to release their full pungency.

1 Cook the diced sweet potato in the top of a steamer for about 5 minutes until just tender. Meanwhile, grease a medium tall 6-inch diameter x 3 3/4-inch deep soufflé dish with a little olive oil, then line the dish with the bread crumbs (see page 8). Attach a soufflé collar that stands 3 inches higher than the top of the dish (see page 8).

2 Melt the butter in a pan with the olive oil. Add the crushed seeds and garlic and cook for 1/2 minute. Stir in the flour, then gradually mix in the milk and bring to a boil, stirring until thickened and smooth.

3 Remove the pan from the heat and stir in the egg yolks, turmeric, paprika, and some salt and pepper. Gently stir in the sweet potato and let cool.

4 Beat the egg whites into stiff, moist-looking peaks. Fold a large spoonful into the cooled sauce to loosen the mixture, then fold in the remaining egg whites.

5 Pour the mixture into the prepared soufflé dish and bake in a preheated oven, 375°F, for 25–30 minutes until the soufflé is well risen, the top is browned, and there is a slight wobble to the center.

6 Quickly snip the string off the soufflé collar and gently peel away the paper. Spoon the soufflé onto plates and serve immediately.

minted pea and feta soufflé

2 tablespoons olive oil, plus extra for
   greasing
2 tablespoons ground almonds
2 tablespoons butter
1/2 cup all-purpose flour
1 1/3 cups skim milk
4 eggs, separated
3 oz feta cheese, drained
   and coarsely grated
1 cup frozen peas, defrosted
   and crushed with a fork
3 tablespoons chopped mint
freshly ground black pepper
tomato and onion salad, to serve

Serves 4
Preparation time: 30 minutes
Cooking time: 30–35 minutes

Transform some humble, high-fiber frozen peas into this lightly minted, Greek-inspired soufflé—perfect for a relaxing summer lunch al fresco. Feta cheese has a strong, salty taste, so a little goes a long way and there is no need to add extra salt when seasoning.

1 Grease a medium tall 6-inch diameter x 3 3/4-inch deep soufflé dish with a little olive oil, then line the dish with the ground almonds (see page 8). Attach a soufflé collar that stands 3 inches higher than the top of the dish (see page 8).

2 Melt the butter in a pan with the olive oil. Stir in the flour and cook for 1 minute. Gradually mix in the milk and bring to a boil, stirring until thickened and smooth.

3 Remove the pan from the heat and stir in the egg yolks, crumbled cheese, and a little pepper. Let cool.

4 Beat the egg whites into stiff, moist-looking peaks. Stir the peas and mint into the cooled sauce, then fold in a large spoonful of egg whites to loosen the mixture. Gently fold in the remaining egg whites.

5 Pour the mixture into the prepared soufflé dish and bake in a preheated oven, 375°F, for 25–30 minutes until the soufflé is well risen, the top is browned, and there is a slight wobble to the center.

6 Quickly snip the string off the soufflé collar and gently peel away the paper. Spoon the soufflé onto plates and serve with a tomato and onion salad.

beet, ricotta, and horseradish soufflés

2 tablespoons olive oil, plus extra for
  greasing
3 tablespoons fresh bread crumbs
2 tablespoons butter
1/2 cup all-purpose flour
1 1/3 cups skim milk
4 eggs, separated
4 teaspoons horseradish sauce
4 tablespoons ricotta cheese
2–3 cooked beets in their own juice,
  about 6 oz, drained and coarsely
  grated
salt and freshly ground black pepper

Serves 4
Preparation time: 30 minutes
Cooking time: 20 minutes

*The amazing purple color of these soufflés is guaranteed to get your guests
talking, and they make a great reduced-fat dinner party appetizer.*

1 Grease 4 small 4-inch diameter x 2 1/2-inch deep soufflé dishes with a little olive
  oil, then line the dishes with the bread crumbs (see page 8). Stand the dishes
  on a baking sheet.

2 Melt the butter in a pan with the olive oil. Stir in the flour and cook for
  1 minute. Gradually mix in the milk and bring to a boil, stirring until thickened
  and smooth.

3 Remove the pan from the heat and stir in the egg yolks and horseradish sauce,
  then the ricotta, grated beets, and some salt and pepper. Let cool.

4 Beat the egg whites into stiff, moist-looking peaks. Fold a large spoonful into the
  cooled sauce to loosen the mixture, then gently fold in the remaining egg whites.

5 Spoon the mixture into the prepared soufflé dishes and bake in a preheated oven,
  375°F, for 15 minutes until the soufflés are well risen, their tops are browned, and
  there is a slight wobble to the centers. Serve immediately.

sage, scallion, and raisin soufflés

2 tablespoons olive oil, plus extra for
   greasing
3 tablespoons fresh bread crumbs
2 tablespoons butter
1/2 cup all-purpose flour
1 1/3 cups skim milk
4 eggs, separated
1/4 cup raisins
5 scallions, thinly sliced
3 tablespoons chopped sage
salt and freshly ground black pepper

Serves 4
Preparation time: 30 minutes
Cooking time: 20 minutes

This is an unusual combination of flavors, but one that works well. To ring the changes, use the same amount of chopped sun-dried tomatoes in oil instead of the raisins or 3–4 oz of blue cheese, depending on its strength. If you don't have any fresh sage, then mix a little dried sage with some freshly chopped parsley.

1 Grease 4 small 4-inch diameter x 2 1/2-inch deep soufflé dishes with a little olive oil, then line the dishes with the bread crumbs (see page 8). Stand the dishes on a baking sheet.

2 Melt the butter in a pan with the olive oil. Stir in the flour and cook for 1 minute. Gradually mix in the milk and bring to a boil, stirring until thickened and smooth.

3 Remove the pan from the heat and stir in the egg yolks, raisins, scallions, sage, and some salt and pepper. Let cool.

4 Beat the egg whites into stiff, moist-looking peaks. Fold a large spoonful into the cooled sauce to loosen the mixture, then gently fold in the remaining egg whites.

5 Spoon the mixture into the prepared soufflé dishes and bake in a preheated oven, 375°F, for 15 minutes until the soufflés are well risen, their tops are browned, and there is a slight wobble to the centers. Serve immediately.

hot date and dark chocolate soufflé

This incredibly rich, dark soufflé is irresistible. No one would guess that it's made with dates for natural sweetness and skim milk.

1 Lightly butter a medium tall 6-inch diameter x 3³/4-inch deep soufflé dish, then line the dish with the ground almonds (see page 8). Attach a soufflé collar that stands 3 inches higher than the top of the dish (see page 8).

2 Put the dates and the water in a small pan, cover, and simmer for 5 minutes until soft. Let cool.

3 Meanwhile, beat the egg yolks and superfine sugar in a bowl until thick, pale, and mousse-like. Sift the flour over the surface, then gently fold it in.

4 Bring the milk just to a boil in a separate pan, then gradually beat it into the egg yolk mixture. Return the milk mixture to the pan and cook over medium heat, stirring continuously until thickened and smooth. Remove from the heat, add the chocolate, and stir until melted. Mix in the dates, then let cool.

5 Beat the egg whites into stiff, moist-looking peaks. Fold a large spoonful into the cooled sauce to loosen the mixture, then gently fold in the remaining egg whites.

6 Spoon the mixture into the prepared soufflé dish and bake in a preheated oven, 400°F, for 25–30 minutes until the soufflé is well risen, the top is browned, and there is a slight wobble to the center.

7 Quickly snip the string off the soufflé collar and gently peel away the paper. Dust the top of the soufflé with sifted confectioners' sugar and cocoa and serve immediately.

butter, for greasing
2 tablespoons ground almonds
1/3 cup finely chopped pitted dried
    dates
4 tablespoons water
3 egg yolks
2 tablespoons superfine sugar
1/3 cup all-purpose flour
1 cup skim milk
4 oz bittersweet chocolate, broken into
    pieces
5 egg whites
sifted confectioners' sugar and
    unsweetened cocoa, for dusting

Serves 4
Preparation time: 30 minutes
Cooking time: 35–40 minutes

crushed lime, coconut, and mango soufflés

4 tablespoons water

4 teaspoons powdered gelatin

4 eggs, separated

1/4 cup superfine sugar

3 teaspoons cornstarch

14-fl oz can reduced-fat coconut milk

1 large mango, peeled, seeded, and
    chopped

grated zest and juice of 2 limes

coarsely chopped and halved pistachio
    nuts, to decorate

Serves 6

Preparation time: 30 minutes, plus
    chilling

Cooking time: 10 minutes

*Completely dairy free, this chilled soufflé is made with a coconut milk custard,
flavored with lime zest and juice, then mixed with a purée of fresh mango and
lightened with beaten egg whites.*

1 Attach soufflé collars to 6 individual 3-inch diameter x 1 1/2-inch deep soufflé
dishes so that the paper stands 1 1/2 inches higher than the top of each dish
(see page 8). Stand the dishes on a tray.

2 Put the water in a small heatproof bowl or mug and sprinkle over the gelatin,
making sure that the water absorbs all the powder. Set aside for 5 minutes.

3 Beat the egg yolks, sugar, and cornstarch in a bowl until thick and pale. Bring
the coconut milk just to a boil in a pan, then gradually beat it into the egg yolk
mixture. Return the milk mixture to the pan.

4 Cook the coconut custard over medium heat, stirring continuously until it is
thickened and smooth and the custard coats the back of the wooden spoon.
Remove from the heat, add the soaked gelatin, and stir until it has completely
dissolved. Let cool.

5 Blend the chopped mango in a blender or food processor until smooth. Stir into
the coconut custard with the lime zest and juice and chill in the refrigerator until
it is just beginning to set. (If the custard seems to be taking a long time to
thicken in the refrigerator, transfer it to the freezer for 10–15 minutes.)

6 Beat the egg whites into stiff, moist-looking peaks. Fold a large spoonful into
the setting coconut custard to loosen the mixture, then gently fold in the
remaining egg whites. Pour the mixture into the prepared soufflé dishes so that
it stands above the rim of the dishes. Chill for 4 hours or until set.

7 To serve, snip the string off the soufflé collars and gently peel away the paper.
Press the chopped pistachio nuts around the sides of the soufflés with a knife
and arrange a few nut halves on top, to decorate.

warm vanilla and prune soufflés

butter, for greasing
3 tablespoons ground almonds
1 vanilla bean
1 cup skim milk
3 egg yolks
1/4 cup superfine sugar
1/3 cup all-purpose flour
5 egg whites
1 cup ready-to-eat pitted prunes,
    finely chopped
sifted confectioners' sugar, for dusting

Serves 4
Preparation time: 30 minutes
Cooking time: 15–17 minutes

Well known for being rich in fiber, prunes are also naturally sweet so that the amount of sugar in this soufflé is less than usual. While this doesn't affect the finished flavor, it helps to reduce the calories greatly in this very tasty dessert.

1 Lightly butter 4 small 4-inch diameter x 2 1/2-inch deep soufflé dishes, then line the dishes with the ground almonds (see page 8). Stand the dishes on a baking sheet.

2 Cut a slit along the length of the vanilla bean, then place it in a pan with the milk and bring just to a boil. Set aside for 15 minutes for the vanilla flavor to develop.

3 Beat the egg yolks and superfine sugar in a bowl until thick, pale, and mousse-like. Sift the flour over the surface, then gently fold it in.

4 Lift the vanilla bean out of the milk, scrape the black seeds from the inside of the pod, and add to the milk. Reheat the milk, then gradually beat it into the egg yolk mixture. Return the milk mixture to the pan and heat, stirring continuously until thickened and smooth. Let cool.

5 Beat the egg whites into stiff, moist-looking peaks. Stir the chopped prunes into the cooled sauce, then fold in a large spoonful of egg whites to loosen the mixture. Gently fold in the remaining egg whites.

6 Spoon the mixture into the prepared soufflé dishes and bake in a preheated oven, 425°F, for 10–12 minutes until the soufflés are well risen, their tops are browned, and there is a slight wobble to the centers. Dust the tops of the soufflés liberally with sifted confectioners' sugar and serve immediately.

saffron and smooth apricot soufflé

1 cup ready-to-eat dried apricots
1/4 teaspoon saffron threads
2/3 cup water, plus 4 tablespoons
4 teaspoons powdered gelatin
4 eggs, separated
1/4 cup superfine sugar
1 cup low-fat plain yogurt

Serves 6
Preparation time: 30 minutes, plus
    chilling
Cooking time: 23–24 minutes

This pretty, pale orange-colored chilled soufflé combines the flavor of apricots with a subtle hint of saffron. Although low-fat yogurt is used here in place of heavy cream, the flavor is just as good.

1 Attach a soufflé collar to a small 5¹/₂-inch diameter x 2¹/₂-inch deep soufflé dish so that the paper stands 2¹/₂ inches higher than the top of the dish (see page 8).

2 Put the apricots, saffron, and the ²/₃ cup of water in a small pan, cover, and simmer for 10 minutes until softened. Blend in a blender or food processor until smooth and let cool.

3 Put the remaining water in a small heatproof bowl or mug and sprinkle over the gelatin, making sure that the water absorbs all the powder. Set aside for 5 minutes, then stand the bowl in a small pan half-filled with boiling water and simmer for 3–4 minutes, stirring occasionally, until the gelatin dissolves to a clear liquid.

4 Put the egg yolks and sugar in a large heatproof bowl, then stand the bowl over a pan of simmering water so that the bottom of the bowl is not touching the water. Beat using a hand-held electric beater for about 10 minutes until the eggs are very thick and pale, and the beater leaves a trail when lifted above the mixture. Remove the bowl from the heat and continue beating until cool.

5 Gradually fold in the dissolved gelatin, adding it in a thin, steady stream, then fold in the apricot purée and the yogurt. Chill until just beginning to set.

6 Beat the egg whites into stiff, moist-looking peaks. Fold a large spoonful into the apricot mixture to loosen it, then gently fold in the remaining egg whites. Pour the mixture into the prepared soufflé dish so that it stands above the rim of the dish. Chill for 4 hours or until set. To serve, snip the string off the soufflé collar and gently peel away the paper.

honeyed banana soufflés with fresh figs

4 tablespoons water

4 teaspoons powdered gelatin

4 eggs, separated

3 tablespoons thick-set flower honey

2 bananas, about 13 oz, in total,
weighed with skins on

2 tablespoons freshly squeezed lemon
juice

1 cup low-fat strained plain yogurt

To decorate

1/2 cup slivered almonds, toasted and
coarsely chopped (optional)

1 fresh fig, cut into 6 wedges

Serves 6

Preparation time: 30 minutes, plus
chilling

Cooking time: 13–14 minutes

Thick-set flower honey is used here for its superior flavor and mixed with strained plain yogurt and naturally sweet ripe bananas for a delicate, fresh-tasting chilled soufflé. The soufflé tops have been decorated with wedges of fresh fig, but slices of banana dipped in lemon juice or a few fresh raspberries could be used instead.

1   Attach soufflé collars to 6 individual 3-inch diameter x 1½-inch deep soufflé dishes so that the paper stands 1½ inches higher than the top of each dish (see page 8).

2   Put the water in a small heatproof bowl or mug and sprinkle over the gelatin, making sure that the water absorbs all the powder. Set aside for 5 minutes, then stand the bowl in a small pan half-filled with boiling water and simmer for 3–4 minutes, stirring occasionally, until the gelatin dissolves to a clear liquid.

3   Put the egg yolks and honey in a large heatproof bowl, then stand the bowl over a pan of simmering water so that the bottom of the bowl is not touching the water. Beat using a hand-held electric beater for about 10 minutes until the eggs are very thick and pale, and the beater leaves a trail when lifted above the mixture. Remove the bowl from the heat and continue beating until cool.

4   Gradually fold in the dissolved gelatin, adding it in a thin, steady stream. Mash the bananas on a plate with the lemon juice, then fold into the egg yolk mixture with the yogurt.

5   Beat the egg whites into stiff, moist-looking peaks. Fold a large spoonful into the mixture to loosen it, then gently fold in the remaining egg whites. Spoon the mixture into the prepared soufflé dishes so that it stands above the rim of the dishes. Chill for 4 hours or until set.

6   To serve, snip the string off the soufflé collars and gently peel away the paper. Press the toasted almonds, if using, around the sides of the soufflés with a knife and arrange the fig wedges on top, to decorate.

soufflés with
a difference

mushroom and pancetta soufflé omelet

1 tablespoon olive oil

6 oz mixed wild or cup mushrooms, sliced

4 oz pancetta or ham, diced

3 tablespoons full-fat crème fraîche or sour cream

4 teaspoons chopped thyme

4 eggs, separated

1/2 teaspoon Dijon mustard

1 1/2 tablespoons butter

salt and freshly ground black pepper

mixed salad, to serve

Serves 2
Preparation time: 15 minutes
Cooking time: 10–12 minutes

This recipe transforms simple eggs and bacon into a supper dish that is more sophisticated, but doesn't take much longer to make. Unlike other omelets, a soufflé omelet does not require stirring during cooking.

1 Heat the oil in a large skillet, add the mushrooms and pancetta or ham, and fry for 5 minutes, stirring frequently until golden. Stir in the crème fraîche or sour cream and thyme, then slide the mixture out of the pan and keep hot.

2 Wash and dry the pan. Beat the egg whites into stiff, moist-looking peaks. Mix together the egg yolks, mustard, and salt and pepper, then fold into the egg whites.

3 Heat the butter in the skillet, add the egg mixture, and cook over medium heat for 3–4 minutes until the underside is golden. Quickly transfer the pan to a hot broiler and cook for 2–3 minutes until the top is brown and the center still slightly soft, making sure that the handle is away from the heat.

4 Spoon the mushroom and pancetta mixture over the omelet, and fold in half. Serve immediately with a mixed salad.

sweet soufflé omelet with strawberries

2 1/4 cups strawberries, hulled and
   thickly sliced, plus extra to decorate
2 tablespoons redcurrant jelly
2 teaspoons balsamic vinegar
5 eggs, separated
4 tablespoons confectioners' sugar,
   sifted

Serves 4
Preparation time: 15 minutes
Cooking time: 8–10 minutes

Balsamic vinegar is a surprising addition to this recipe, but its slight sharpness helps to reduce the richness of the light, fluffy, cloud-like sweet omelet. Make and serve this omelet at the very last minute for maximum volume.

1 Warm the sliced strawberries, redcurrant jelly, and vinegar together in a pan until the jelly has just melted.

2 Meanwhile, beat the egg whites into stiff, moist-looking peaks. Mix the egg yolks with 1 tablespoon of the sugar, then fold into the egg whites.

3 Heat the butter in a large skillet, add the egg mixture, and cook over medium heat for 3–4 minutes until the underside is golden. Quickly transfer the pan to a hot broiler and cook for 2–3 minutes until the top is browned and the center still slightly soft, making sure that the handle is away from the heat.

4 Spoon the warm strawberry mixture over the omelet, fold in half, and dust with the remaining sugar. Cut into 4 and serve with extra strawberries.

iced strawberry daiquiri soufflé

This gelatin-free soufflé is made with a base of Italian meringue, a stiff meringue that is mixed with a hot sugar syrup rather than oven baked, and flavored with whipped heavy cream and the traditional daiquiri ingredients of lime and white rum.

3 cups fresh strawberries, hulled,
   plus extra halved or quartered,
   depending on size, to decorate
1 cup superfine sugar
1 tablespoon liquid glucose
3 tablespoons water
4 eggs, separated
1 cup heavy cream
finely grated zest and juice of 2 limes
4 tablespoons white rum

Serves 6–8
Preparation time: 40 minutes, plus
   freezing
Cooking time: 10 minutes

1 Attach a soufflé collar to a medium 6³/₄-inch diameter x 3-inch deep soufflé dish so that the paper stands 3 inches higher than the top of the dish (see page 8).

2 Blend the strawberries in a blender or food processor until smooth, then press through a strainer.

3 Gently heat the sugar, liquid glucose, and water in a small pan, without stirring, until the sugar has completely dissolved. Add a candy thermometer and heat to 230°F, still without stirring.

4 Meanwhile, put the egg whites in a large bowl. When the candy thermometer reaches the required temperature, begin beating the egg whites and continue heating the sugar syrup to 250°F.

5 Once the temperature is reached, begin to pour the boiling syrup slowly into the egg whites as you beat. Continue beating for 10–15 minutes until the meringue mixture has cooled.

6 Softly whip the cream, then add the lime zest and gradually beat in the juice and rum. Fold in the strawberry purée.

7 Fold the strawberry mixture into the meringue mixture, one-third at a time, until completely mixed. Pour the mixture into the prepared soufflé dish so that it stands above the rim of the dish. Freeze overnight until firm.

8 To serve, snip the string off the soufflé collar and gently peel away the paper. Decorate the top with extra strawberries. Scoop immediately from the dish using a warmed spoon.

gingered chocolate roulade

5 eggs, separated
3/4 cup superfine sugar, plus extra for
   dusting
7 oz bittersweet chocolate, melted
2 tablespoons warm water

Filling
1 cup heavy cream
2 tablespoons chopped
   crystallized ginger

To decorate
chocolate curls (see method)
sifted confectioners' sugar, for dusting

Serves 6–8
Preparation time: 40 minutes, plus
   cooling
Cooking time: 15–20 minutes

This popular Christmas dessert can be made and frozen in advance. For a summer version, add fresh raspberries or strawberries in place of the ginger. The absence of flour makes this especially good for people on a wheat-free diet.

1 Line a 9 x 12-inch roasting pan with parchment paper and snip into the corners so that the paper fits snugly.

2 Beat the egg yolks and superfine sugar in a large bowl until thick and pale, and the beater leaves a trail when lifted above the mixture. Add the melted chocolate and warm water and gently fold together.

3 Wash the beaters and dry well, then use to beat the egg whites into stiff, moist-looking peaks. Fold a large spoonful into the chocolate mixture to loosen it, then gently fold in the remaining egg whites.

4 Spoon the mixture into the prepared pan and ease it into the corners. Bake the roulade in a preheated oven, 350°F, for 15–20 minutes until it is well risen and the top feels crusty to the touch. Cover with a clean dish towel and let cool for at least 4 hours.

5 Meanwhile, make the decorative chocolate curls. Run a swivel-blade vegetable peeler along the smooth underside of a bar of bittersweet chocolate. If the curls are very tiny, microwave the bar of chocolate in 15-second bursts until it softens and you can make bigger curls. Set aside.

6 Softly whip the cream, then fold in the crystallized ginger. Wet a clean dish towel, wring out, and place on the countertop so that a short edge is nearest you. Cover with a large piece of parchment paper and sprinkle with a little superfine sugar. Turn the cooled roulade out onto the paper, remove the pan, and peel away the lining paper. Spread the roulade with the gingered cream, then roll it up, starting from the shortest side nearest you, using the sugared paper and dish towel to help.

7 Transfer the roulade to a serving plate, top with chocolate curls, and dust with confectioners' sugar. Cut into thick slices to serve.

hazelnut and pear roulade with mascarpone

1 cup hazelnuts

5 eggs, separated

3/4 cup superfine sugar, plus extra for sprinkling

1 just-ripe pear, peeled and coarsely grated

Filling

1 cup mascarpone cheese

2 tablespoons confectioners' sugar

4–6 fresh apricots, about 8 oz, pitted and coarsely chopped

Serves 6–8

Preparation time: 30 minutes, plus cooling

Cooking time: 18–19 minutes

Toasted hazelnuts, juicy pears, and creamy smooth mascarpone encased in a light-as-air sponge make this an irresistible cake for a special afternoon tea. When fresh apricots are out of season, use a well-drained 13 1/2-oz can of apricot halves instead.

1 Line a 9 x 12-inch roasting pan with parchment paper and snip into the corners so that the paper fits snugly.

2 Put the hazelnuts on a piece of foil and toast under the broiler for 3–4 minutes until golden. Coarsely chop 2 tablespoons and set aside for decoration, then grind the remainder in a food processor until very finely chopped.

3 Beat the egg yolks and superfine sugar in a large bowl until thick and pale, and the beater leaves a trail when lifted above the mixture. Fold the toasted finely chopped hazelnuts and grated pear into the egg yolk mixture.

4 Wash the beaters and dry well, then use to beat the egg whites into stiff, moist-looking peaks. Fold a large spoonful into the nut mixture to loosen it, then gently fold in the remaining egg whites.

5 Spoon the mixture into the prepared pan and ease it into the corners. Bake the roulade in a preheated oven, 350°F, for 15 minutes until it is well risen, golden brown, and the top feels spongy. Cover with a clean dish towel and let cool for at least 1 hour.

6 Beat the mascarpone cheese and confectioners' sugar together until soft. Wet a clean dish towel, wring out, and place on the countertop so that a short edge is nearest you. Cover with a large piece of parchment paper and sprinkle with a little superfine sugar. Turn the cooled roulade out onto the paper, remove the pan, and peel away the lining paper.

7 Spread the roulade with the mascarpone mixture, then sprinkle with the apricots. Roll up the roulade, starting from the shortest side nearest you, using the sugared paper and dish towel to help. Transfer the roulade to a serving plate, sprinkle with the coarsely chopped hazelnuts, and cut into thick slices to serve.

watercress and salmon roulade

3 tablespoons butter

1/3 cup all-purpose flour

1 cup milk

4 eggs, separated

2 cups watercress, coarsely chopped,
    plus a few extra leaves to garnish

grated zest of 1 lime

3 tablespoons ready-grated Parmesan
    cheese

salt and freshly ground black pepper

lime wedges, to garnish

Filling

10 oz salmon fillet, halved

1 cup full-fat crème fraîche or equal
    parts whipping cream and sour
    cream (left to stand for 2–5 hours
    until thickened)

2 tablespoons freshly squeezed lime
    juice

salt and freshly ground black pepper

Serves 4–6

Preparation time: 30 minutes, plus
    cooling

Cooking time: 23–30 minutes

This roulade would be ideal served at a summer wedding anniversary or christening party. If serving it as part of a large buffet, cut it into 10 slices and make two, three, or more the day before required. Refrigerating the finished roulade, tightly wrapped in paper, for at least 30 minutes makes slicing easier.

1 Line a 9 x 12-inch roasting pan with parchment paper and snip into the corners so that the paper fits snugly.

2 Melt the butter in a pan, stir in the flour, and cook for 1 minute. Gradually mix in the milk and bring to a boil, stirring until thickened and smooth. Remove from the heat and stir in the egg yolks, watercress, lime zest, and salt and pepper. Let cool for 15 minutes.

3 Beat the egg whites into stiff, moist-looking peaks. Fold a large spoonful into the cooled sauce to loosen the mixture, then fold in the remaining egg whites. Spoon the mixture into the prepared pan and ease into the corners.

4 Bake the roulade in a preheated oven, 350°F, for 15–20 minutes until it is well risen, golden brown, and the top feels spongy. Cover with a clean dish towel and let cool for at least 1 hour.

5 Meanwhile, steam the salmon for 8–10 minutes until it just flakes and the flakes are the same opaque color all the way through. Let cool, before skinning, flaking, and discarding any bones. Beat the crème fraîche or cream mixture with the lime juice and plenty of salt and pepper.

6 Wet a clean dish towel, wring out, and place on the countertop so that a short edge is nearest you. Cover with a large piece of parchment paper and sprinkle with the Parmesan. Turn the cooled roulade out onto the paper, remove the pan, and peel away the lining paper.

7 Spread the roulade with the crème fraîche or cream mixture, then the salmon. Roll up the roulade, starting from the shortest side nearest you, using the paper and dish towel to help. Cut into thick slices and serve garnished with a few watercress leaves and lime wedges.

spinach and prosciutto roulade

1¹/2 cups frozen leaf spinach,
    defrosted
3 tablespoons butter
¹/3 cup all-purpose flour
1 cup milk
4 eggs, separated
large pinch of grated nutmeg
3 tablespoons ready-grated Parmesan
    cheese
salt and freshly ground black pepper
roasted bell pepper and tomato salad,
    to serve (optional)

Filling
1 cup cream cheese with garlic
    and herbs, stirred to soften
6 slices of prosciutto

Serves 4–6
Preparation time: 30 minutes, plus
    cooling
Cooking time: 15–20 minutes

If you have time, roll up the filled roulade an hour or so before you need it, then keep it wrapped in nonstick parchment paper to set the shape and make slicing easier. For vegetarians, substitute thin slices of bottled red pimiento for the prosciutto.

1 Line a 9 x 12-inch roasting pan with parchment paper and snip into the corners so that the paper fits snugly. Put the spinach in a strainer set over a bowl and press out any water using the back of a spoon.

2 Melt the butter in a pan, stir in the flour, and cook for 1 minute. Gradually mix in the milk and bring to a boil, stirring until thickened and smooth. Remove the pan from the heat and stir in the spinach, egg yolks, nutmeg, and salt and pepper. Let cool for 15 minutes.

3 Beat the egg whites into stiff, moist-looking peaks. Fold a large spoonful into the cooled sauce to loosen the mixture, then gently fold in the remaining egg whites. Spoon the mixture into the prepared pan and ease into the corners.

4 Bake the roulade in a preheated oven, 350°F, for 15–20 minutes until it is well risen, golden brown, and the top feels spongy. Cover with a clean dish towel and let cool for at least 1 hour.

5 Wet a clean dish towel, wring out, and place on the countertop so that a short edge is nearest you. Cover with a large piece of parchment paper and sprinkle with the Parmesan. Turn the cooled roulade out onto the paper, remove the pan, and peel away the lining paper.

6 Spread the roulade with the cream cheese and cover with slices of prosciutto. Roll up the roulade, starting from the shortest side nearest you, using the paper and dish towel to help. Cut into thick slices and serve 1 slice per person for an appetizer or 2 for a light supper with a roasted bell pepper and tomato salad.

shrimp, gruyère, and leek roulade

3 tablespoons butter
1/3 cup all-purpose flour
1 cup milk
4 eggs, separated
3/4 cup grated Gruyère cheese
1 teaspoon Dijon mustard
10 oz frozen cooked shelled shrimp,
     just defrosted, rinsed, and well
     drained
2 tablespoons ready-grated Parmesan
     cheese

Filling
2 tablespoons butter
1 tablespoon olive oil
14 oz leeks, slit, well rinsed, and
     very thinly sliced
salt and freshly ground black pepper

Serves 4–6
Preparation time: 30 minutes
Cooking time: 19–25 minutes

This very tasty cheesy roulade dotted with shrimp is filled with a green ribbon of sautéed leeks. Serve with new potatoes for a supper dish or as a sophisticated dinner party dish served in a pool of warmed canned lobster bisque.

1 Line a 9 x 12-inch roasting pan with parchment paper and snip into the corners so that the paper fits snugly.

2 Melt the butter in a pan, stir in the flour, and cook for 1 minute. Gradually mix in the milk and bring to a boil, stirring until thickened and smooth. Remove the pan from the heat and stir in the egg yolks, cheese, mustard, and salt and pepper. Let cool for 15 minutes.

3 Beat the egg whites into stiff, moist-looking peaks. Fold the shrimp into the cooled sauce, then a large spoonful of egg whites to loosen the mixture. Gently fold in the remaining egg whites. Spoon the mixture into the prepared pan and ease into the corners.

4 Bake the roulade in a preheated oven, 350°F, for 15–20 minutes until it is well risen, golden brown, and the top feels spongy. Meanwhile, make the leek filling. Heat the butter and oil in a skillet, add the leeks, and sauté for 4–5 minutes, stirring frequently, until softened. Season with salt and pepper.

5 Wet a clean dish towel, wring out, and place on the countertop so that a short edge is nearest you. Cover with a large piece of parchment paper and sprinkle with the Parmesan. Turn the hot roulade out onto the paper, remove the pan, and peel away the lining paper. Cover the roulade with the hot leeks and roll up, starting from the shortest side nearest you, using the paper and dish towel to help.

6 Cut the roulade into thick slices and serve 1 slice per person for an appetizer or 2 for a light supper.

cheese and sun-blushed tomato soufflé tart

1½ tablespoons butter, plus extra for
   greasing
12 oz short-crust pie dough, defrosted
   if frozen
2½ tablespoons all-purpose flour
2/3 cup milk
3 eggs, separated
2 teaspoons chopped rosemary
4 oz individual goat cheeses, diced
2 teaspoons Dijon mustard
3½ oz sun-blushed tomatoes in
   oil, drained and sliced
salt and freshly ground black pepper

Serves 6
Preparation time: 40 minutes, plus
   chilling
Cooking time: 45–50 minutes
Chilling time: 15 minutes

*Rather than simply forking together eggs and milk for a tart filling, here the eggs
have been separated and beaten for extra volume and lightness, then flavored with
goat cheese and rosemary and baked over a layer of sun-blushed tomatoes.*

1 Lightly butter a 9-inch deep loose-bottom tart pan. Roll the pie dough out thinly
on a lightly floured countertop until a little larger than the pan, then lift over a
rolling pin into the pan. Press into the bottom and sides, trim off the excess
dough, and prick the base with a fork. Chill for 15 minutes.

2 Line the tart shell with a piece of waxed or parchment paper and ceramic
baking beans. Set on a baking sheet and bake in a preheated oven, 375°F, for
10 minutes. Remove the paper and beans and cook for 5 more minutes until
golden brown around the edges.

3 Meanwhile, melt the butter in a pan, stir in the flour, and cook for 1 minute.
Gradually mix in the milk and bring to a boil, stirring until thickened and smooth.
Remove from the heat and stir in the egg yolks, rosemary, goat cheese, and salt
and pepper. Let cool for 15 minutes.

4 Spread the bottom of the tart shell with the mustard and cover with the sliced
sun-blushed tomatoes.

5 Beat the egg whites into stiff, moist-looking peaks. Fold a large spoonful into
the cooled sauce to loosen the mixture, then gently fold in the remaining egg
whites. Spoon the mixture into the tart shell and bake for 25–30 minutes until
golden brown and just set. Serve warm, cut into wedges.

double chocolate soufflé tart

Pie dough
1 1/2 cups all-purpose flour
2 tablespoons unsweetened cocoa
1/4 cup superfine sugar
1/2 cup butter, diced, plus extra
    for greasing
2 1/2–3 tablespoons water

Filling
4 oz white chocolate, broken
    into pieces
2 tablespoons butter
4 eggs, separated
1/3 cup superfine sugar
grated zest of 1/2 orange
3 oz bittersweet chocolate, chopped

To decorate
confectioners' sugar, for dusting
white chocolate curls (see page 61)
orange zest curls (see page 57)

orange segments, to serve

Serves 6
Preparation time: 40 minutes, plus
    chilling
Cooking time: 35 minutes

This is perhaps not a true soufflé, but one that combines all the traditional elements of beaten yolks and sugar gently folded with light-as-air beaten whites, flavored with melted white chocolate and encased in a rich, dark, buttery chocolate pie crust.

1 To make the pie dough, put the flour, cocoa, superfine sugar, and butter in a bowl and cut in the butter until the mixture resembles fine crumbs. Stir in enough of the water to make a smooth, soft dough. Knead lightly, then roll out on a lightly floured countertop and use to line a 9-inch buttered, loose-bottom tart pan. Trim off the excess dough, prick the bottom with a fork, and chill for 15 minutes.

2 Line the tart shell with a piece of waxed or parchment paper and ceramic baking beans. Set on a baking sheet and bake in a preheated oven, 375°F, for 10 minutes. Remove the paper and beans and cook for 5 more minutes.

3 Reduce the oven temperature to 350°F. Melt the white chocolate and butter in a large heatproof bowl set over a pan of just-boiled water.

4 Make the filling by beating the egg yolks, superfine sugar, and orange zest in a large bowl until thick and pale, and the beater leaves a trail when lifted above the mixture. Fold in the melted chocolate and butter.

5 Wash the beater and dry well, then use to beat the egg whites into stiff, moist-looking peaks. Fold a large spoonful into the white chocolate mixture to loosen it, then fold in the remaining egg whites.

6 Sprinkle the dark chocolate onto the bottom of the tart shell, then cover with the white chocolate mixture. Bake for 20 minutes until the filling is well risen, the top feels crusty, and there is a slight wobble to the center. Check after 15 minutes and cover lightly with foil if the filling seems to be browning too quickly. Let cool—as the tart cools, the filling will sink slightly.

7 Remove the tart from the pan and place on a serving plate. Dust with confectioners' sugar and top with white chocolate curls. Serve, cut into wedges, with some orange segments.

index

acknowledgments

Photography Lis Parsons
Food Styling Sara Lewis